THE SCANDINAVIAN
WAY TO COOK

NICHE BOOKS

Le Creuset is delighted to introduce 'The Scandinavian Way to Cook', the first book that brings together all of our premium cookware ranges in a celebration of the inspiring cuisine of Scandinavia.

Each chapter leads you through a season of honest Nordic cooking, using the very freshest ingredients in 40 delicious recipes. From hearty soups and generous loaves of bread, to succulent meat dishes, fish and seafood, traditional to the Nordic coastlines, and tempting desserts, all recipes use seasonal fruits, vegetables and herbs throughout. The recipes also make the most of the pickling, brining and curing that are central to Scandinavian cooking.

Known for their distinctive rugged, unspoiled beauty and natural wide open spaces, Nordic countries have been enjoying somewhat of a gastronomic revival over the past decade, in a world constantly hungry for new tastes and food experiences. Le Creuset has long been a leader in producing the very best cookware and 'The Scandinavian Way to Cook' shows how our Scandinavian recipes can be cooked and served to perfection for those who want to recreate global food trends at home. Whether you choose to bake, boil, sauté or roast, there is a piece of Le Creuset to suit every culinary requirement, offering superb versatility in shape and size, cooking styles and recipes.

Renowned as the undisputed cookware of choice for over 85 years, innovation has always remained at the forefront of the Le Creuset success story. Throughout that time, our world famous Le Creuset Cast Iron collection has been manufactured at our foundry in the small town of Fresnoy-le-Grand, Northern France. Although the original signature enamelled Cast Iron cookware remains at the core of our cookware collection, we now also offer two additional premium cookware ranges; the high-performance 3-ply Stainless Steel cookware collection and the Toughened Non-Stick range which features our ultimate, super-durable non-stick coating. To complement the Le Creuset cookware offering is the Stoneware oven-to-table range plus a whole host of professional kitchen accessories too. All Le Creuset cookware products come with the reassurance of a lifetime guarantee, and Le Creuset Stoneware oven-to-tableware with a 5-year guarantee, so you can be secure in the knowledge that you are cooking with the best.

So whether you are a long-time lover of Scandinavian cooking or a first timer keen to taste the delights of Northern European gastronomy, this book is a great way to bring Nordic cuisine into your home. We hope that 'The Scandinavian Way to Cook' will become a favourite that you will return to again and again.

SPRING

11 SPELT BLINIS
WITH LUMPFISH CAVIAR, HERBS AND CITRUS CRÈME FRAÎCHE

12 WOK-FRIED TIGER PRAWNS
WITH EGG NOODLES, SPROUTS, GINGER AND SPRING CABBAGE

15 FJORD PRAWN SOUP
WITH GARLIC YOGHURT AND GRILLED BREAD

16 OPEN RAVIOLI
WITH HERBS, RICOTTA, MUSHROOMS, PARMESAN AND BROWNED BUTTER

19 FISHCAKES
WITH FRESH REMOULADE AND NEW POTATOES

20 SPRING SALAD
WITH SPINACH, PEAS, ASPARAGUS AND LEMON YOGHURT

23 FOCACCIA
WITH ROSEMARY, OLIVE AND SEA SALT

24 PANCAKES
WITH LEMON-INFUSED STRAWBERRIES AND POPPY SEEDS

27 CHOCOLATE FONDUE
WITH STRAWBERRIES AND PINEAPPLE

SPELT BLINIS

WITH LUMPFISH CAVIAR, HERBS AND CITRUS CRÈME FRAÎCHE

APPETISER – SERVES 4

BLINIS: 150G WHEAT FLOUR · 50G SPELT FLOUR · 2 TSP DRY YEAST · 200ML LOW-FAT MILK
2 EGGS, YOLKS AND WHITE SEPARATED · 200ML PLAIN YOGHURT · ¼ BUNCH OR 10G FLAT-LEAF PARSLEY
50G BUTTER · 1 TSP SALT · BLACK PEPPER

250ML CRÈME FRAÎCHE · 1 TBS LEMON JUICE · 1 TSP FINELY-GRATED LEMON ZEST
50G LUMPFISH CAVIAR · ¼ BUNCH OR 10G DILL · ¼ BUNCH OR 10G CHIVES
FRESHLY-GROUND BLACK PEPPER

To make the blini batter mix together the flour, dry yeast, salt and pepper in a large bowl. Pour the milk into a pan and heat until warm. Whisk the yolks with the milk, yoghurt and the parsley, which should be finely chopped. Stir into the flour mixture gradually to make a smooth batter, then let it rest for 10 minutes. Whisk the egg whites until stiff and fold into the batter. Cook the batter using a blini pan or melt a little of the butter at a time in a large non-stick frying pan and cook individually.

Whip the crème fraîche until stiff, then fold the lemon juice and lemon zest into the creamy mixture.

Dress the small blinis with crème fraîche, lumpfish caviar, dill, chives and black pepper.

{ Lumpfish caviar is fantastic at this time of year, but salmon roe and other similar roe products can easily be substituted as an alternative. }

WOK-FRIED TIGER PRAWNS

WITH EGG NOODLES, SPROUTS, GINGER AND SPRING CABBAGE

SERVES 4

400G EGG NOODLES · 400G SPRING GREENS · 50G GINGER · 24 TIGER PRAWNS, RAW AND PEELED
2 CLOVES GARLIC · 2 ONIONS · 2 TBS SUNFLOWER OIL · 100G BEAN SPROUTS
SALT AND FRESHLY-GROUND PEPPER

Put the noodles into a large bowl and pour boiling water over them. Soak the noodles for 20 minutes, then drain in a sieve and place into a warmed bowl. You can also boil the noodles according to the directions on the pack. Cut the spring greens into small pieces, roughly 3x3cm, and cut the ginger into strips.

Finely chop the garlic and onions. Heat the oil in the wok or frying pan, add the garlic and onions and cook until they are lightly browned. Add the ginger, prawns and cabbage, and fry at a high temperature for 3-4 minutes, adding the sprouts for the final minute. Add the prawns, vegetables and herbs into the hot noodles and mix well. Add salt and pepper to taste. Serve in petite casseroles / mini cocottes with chopsticks.

 Soy sauce and freshly chopped coriander enhance the flavour of this dish and give it that little something extra.

FJORD PRAWN SOUP

WITH GARLIC YOGHURT AND GRILLED BREAD

SERVES 4 - 6

500G NORWEGIAN PRAWNS WITH SHELLS · 1 CLOVE GARLIC · 3 ONIONS · 3 TBS OLIVE OIL
4 CARROTS · ½ CELERY STICK · 1 FENNEL BULB, OPTIONAL · 6 TOMATOES · ½ BOTTLE WHITE WINE
2 LITRES WATER · LEMON JUICE · SALT AND PEPPER

GRILLED BREAD · YOGHURT · 1 CLOVE GARLIC · CHIVES

Flash-fry the Norwegian prawns, garlic and coarsely-chopped onions at high heat in a pan with olive oil, until the mixture takes on colour. Add the celery and the rest of the vegetables and tomatoes, also coarsely-chopped, and heat for five minutes. Pour in the wine and cook an additional five minutes, until the smell of alcohol from the wine has dissipated. Add the water and simmer for one hour.

Blend the soup with a powerful blender, then strain with a fine sieve. Add lemon juice, salt and pepper to taste.

Serve the soup with bread, yoghurt mixed with crushed garlic and chives, if desired.

{ Langoustines or stone crabs would be good substitutes for Norwegian prawns in this light and delicious spring course. Your local fishmonger can provide you with all three. The soup can also be reduced further to make a strong stock (if doing this take care not to over season or the end result will be too salty) which could then be used for a delicious shellfish sauce. }

OPEN RAVIOLI

WITH HERBS, RICOTTA, MUSHROOMS, PARMESAN AND BROWNED BUTTER

SERVES 4

2 LARGE LASAGNE SHEETS (FRESH) OR 4 SMALL SHEETS (DRIED) · 30 BASIL LEAVES · 100G RICOTTA CHEESE
50G GRATED PARMESAN DIVIDED · SALT AND PEPPER · 60G BUTTER · 4 FRESH THYME LEAVES
200G RINSED MUSHROOMS

Boil the lasagne sheets in a large pot with plenty of lightly salted water. Remove them while they are still al dente, and put them into a bowl of cold water. Take them out and place them onto a baking sheet covered with baking paper that has been brushed with olive oil. Cut the large sheets into four pieces or small sheets into two.

Chop the basil and stir into the ricotta cheese along with 30g of the grated parmesan, season to taste with salt and pepper. Spread the ricotta mix onto one half of each lasagne sheet, then close the other half over on itself, so it becomes an open ravioli. Bake in a pre-heated oven at 180°C/350°F/Gas Mark 4 for 10 minutes.

Melt the butter in a small saucepan until it browns, then add the thyme. Let it bubble, then remove from the heat. Flash-fry the mushrooms in a little olive oil.

Place the large ravioli on four warm plates. Spread the mushrooms over them, and top with the browned thyme butter. Serve with remaining parmesan.

FISHCAKES

WITH FRESH REMOULADE AND NEW POTATOES

SERVES 4

FISHCAKES: 450G WHITE FISH: COD OR HADDOCK, FILLET · 1 ONION, ROUGHLY CHOPPED
2 TBS WHEAT FLOUR · 2 EGGS · 2 TBS CHOPPED DILL, OPTIONAL · 2 TSP VEGETABLE OIL
1 TSP SALT · BLACK PEPPER

REMOULADE: 150G CELERIAC · 150G CARROTS · 2 TBS MAYONNAISE · 2 TBS CAPERS
100ML YOGHURT · SALT AND PEPPER

SIDE INGREDIENTS: BOILED NEW POTATOES · DILL · LEMONS

Inspect the fish thoroughly for bones, then cut into small pieces. Mince or lightly process the fish and onions and mix well with flour in a bowl. Add one egg at a time, then the chopped dill, and finally add salt and pepper to taste. Shape the mixture into small cakes and pan-fry the fish cakes in a little oil for about three minutes on each side.

To make the remoulade peel and grate the carrots and celeriac into a ramekin, stir in the mayonnaise with the chopped capers and yoghurt, season to taste with salt and pepper.

Serve the warm fishcakes with raw remoulade, potatoes and lemon wedges.

SPRING SALAD

WITH SPINACH, PEAS, ASPARAGUS AND LEMON YOGHURT

SERVES 4

LEMON YOGHURT: 200ML PLAIN YOGHURT · 1 ORGANIC LEMON, JUICE AND FINELY-GRATED ZEST
2 TBS ROASTED PUMPKIN SEEDS · SALT AND PEPPER

12 GREEN ASPARAGUS SPEARS · 8 RADISHES · 200G BOILED CARROTS · ¼ BUNCH OR 10G DILL
150G FRESH PEAS · 100G BABY SPINACH

Stir the juice and zest from the lemon into the yoghurt, and add salt and pepper to taste.

Cut three centimetres off the bottom of the asparagus and slice them finely. Cut the radishes lengthwise, and the carrots into sticks. Chop the dill coarsely. Mix all the vegetables together with spinach and dill, and serve in a large salad bowl with lemon yoghurt and roasted pumpkin seeds.

FOCACCIA

WITH ROSEMARY, OLIVE AND SEA SALT

1 LOAF

500ML COLD WATER · 20G FRESH YEAST · 1 TBS SALT · 3 TBS OLIVE OIL
4 LARGE ROSEMARY SPRIGS · 600G WHEAT FLOUR

Blend the yeast in some of the water then add the remainder, followed by salt, oil and finely-cut rosemary. Gradually add flour while stirring thoroughly. (Note that the dough is wet – this is intentional.) Let the dough rise in the refrigerator for at least six hours, but preferably overnight. By the time it is ready, the dough will have doubled in size.

Prove the bread for 30 minutes at room temperature in a baking dish greased with oil. Cover and bake in a pre-heated oven at 200°C/400°F/Gas Mark 6 for 30-35 minutes. Check the bread's progress by tapping it; if the loaf sounds hollow then it is done. Handle the bread carefully when moving it to a wire cooking tray to cool.

PANCAKES

WITH LEMON-INFUSED STRAWBERRIES AND POPPY SEEDS

SERVES 4, APPROX. 16 PANCAKES

150G WHEAT FLOUR · 2 TBS POPPY SEEDS, OPTIONAL · 1 TBS CANE SUGAR · 1 PINCH SALT
2 TSP BAKING POWDER · 250ML BUTTERMILK/MILK · 1 BEATEN EGG · BUTTER FOR COOKING

TOPPING INGREDIENTS: 200G STRAWBERRIES · 1 TBS SUGAR · JUICE AND RIND FROM ½ LEMON

Combine the flour, poppy seeds, sugar, baking powder and salt in a bowl and stir. Add the buttermilk gradually and mix until there are no lumps in the batter. Stir in the egg.

Heat the pancake pan adding a little butter and cook the pancakes on both sides.

Mix sugar, lemon juice and lemon rind in a bowl. Wash the strawberries, cut them into small pieces and add to the mixture.

Serve the pancakes with the lemon-infused strawberries.

{ Other berries can be substituted when making this hearty dessert.
A scoop of vanilla ice cream would be a delicious addition. }

CHOCOLATE FONDUE

WITH STRAWBERRIES AND PINEAPPLE

SERVES 4

200G DARK CHOCOLATE, 70% COCOA SOLIDS · 200G WHITE CHOCOLATE · 200G STRAWBERRIES
200G PINEAPPLE

DESICCATED COCONUT · SESAME SEEDS · FINELY CHOPPED NUTS

Melt each chocolate separately in a bain-marie. Pour the melted chocolate into small heat-resistant pots and place over a tea-light fondue pot heater.

Wash the fruit and cut into bite sized pieces. To eat, skewer the fruit, dip into the melted chocolate and sprinkle with the side ingredients.

{ Fruit such as bananas, pears, apples and grapes work well in a fondue. }

SUMMER

SMOKED MACKEREL RILLETTES

WITH SUMMER SALAD AND GRILLED BREAD

SERVES 4

1 SMOKED MACKEREL OR 2 FILLETS · ½ BUNCH OR 15G CHIVES · 1 SALAD ONION · 1 SMALL TRAY OF CRESS
8 RADISHES · 2 TBS OLIVE OIL · BREAD · SALT AND PEPPER · 1 LEMON

Remove the skin from the mackerel and remove the meat from the bones. Chop the chives roughly, and thinly slice the salad onion. Clip the cress and halve the radishes.

Mix everything with olive oil, and add salt and pepper to taste. Grill or toast the bread and serve the mackerel rillettes on the grilled bread with lemon.

{ Most types of smoked fish will work for this dish. }

BOILED CRAYFISH

IN NORDIC SUMMER HERBS WITH WILD GARLIC PESTO

SERVES 4

1 KG CRAYFISH · 3 TBS SALT · 1 TBS SUGAR · 4 SPRIGS LOVAGE, OPTIONAL
½ BUNCH OR 15G LEMON THYME · 1 BUNCH OR 30G DILL · 1 UNWAXED LEMON

WILD GARLIC PESTO: 40 BASIL LEAVES · ½ BUNCH OR 15G FLAT-LEAF PARSLEY · 12 WILD GARLIC LEAVES
100 ML OLIVE OIL · 40G TOASTED PINE NUTS · 40G GRATED PARMESAN · SALT AND PEPPER

Cut the lemon into rough pieces and add to a large pan with the sugar, salt, herbs and 4-6 litres of water. Bring the water to the boil and simmer for five minutes. Add the crayfish and simmer for another 10 minutes. Remove the pan and cool the crayfish in the broth.

To make the pesto-chop the basil, parsley and garlic leaves and blend with the oil, add the pine nuts, parmesan cheese and blend again. Season to taste with salt and pepper

Serve the crayfish in a serving bowl with the pesto and bread.

FRIED PLAICE

WITH A SUMMER SALAD OF PEAS, RADISHES, ASPARAGUS AND SMOKED CHEESE

SERVES 4

400-500G PLAICE FILLETS • 2 DILL SPRIGS • 2 TBS BUTTER
SALT AND FRESHLY GROUND BLACK PEPPER

SUMMER SALAD: 100G SMOKED CHEESE • 1 TBS OLIVE OIL • 4 GREEN ASPARAGUS SPEARS
50G FRESH PEAS • 4 RADISHES • 1 BUNCH WATERCRESS

Cube the smoked cheese, cut the radishes and asparagus into slices, mix with the peas and watercress and olive oil and season with salt and pepper. Cut the radishes and asparagus into thin slices and mix with the peas and watercress.

On a chopping board, season the outer side of the fish fillets with coarsely-chopped dill, salt and black pepper.

Fry the fish in a non-stick frying pan with browned butter for about two minutes on each side.

Serve the fish with smoked cheese, summer salad, bread and lemon wedges.

OVEN-BAKED MACARONI

WITH HOT-SMOKED SALMON, CREAM, CHEESE AND CHIVES

SERVES 4

400G WHOLEGRAIN MACARONI · ½ BUNCH OR 15G CHIVES · 300G HOT-SMOKED SALMON
400 ML WHIPPING CREAM · 75G GRATED CHEESE · 2 TBS LEMON JUICE · 1 LEMON
SALT AND FRESHLY GROUND PEPPER

Cook the pasta according to the directions on the pack. Discard the water, and put the pasta into an oven-safe baking dish.

Chop the chives. Skin the salmon and spread it out in the dish (in smaller pieces). Mix the fish and chives into the pasta, and add salt and pepper to taste. Pour in the cream and lemon juice and mix well.

Sprinkle with the grated cheese and bake in a pre-heated oven at 200°C/400°F/Gas Mark 6 until golden and crispy.

Serve in the dish with bread and lemon wedges if desired.

 Breadcrumbs can be mixed with the cheese topping to make the dish extra crispy and delicious. You can also substitute other types of smoked fish or a good smoked ham for the salmon.

THE SCANDINAVIAN WAY TO COOK

SUMMER CHICKEN

WITH TARRAGON, MUSTARD, SPRING ONION, CUCUMBER, LEMON AND NEW POTATOES

SERVES 4

1 SMALL CHICKEN, ABOUT 1 KG · ½ BUNCH OR 15G FRENCH TARRAGON · 2 TBS WHOLEGRAIN MUSTARD
1 TBS DIJON MUSTARD · 2 TBS OLIVE OIL · 800G NEW POTATOES · ½ UNWAXED LEMON
500ML WATER OR CHICKEN STOCK · 250ML WHIPPING CREAM · 1 CUCUMBER
1 BUNCH SPRING ONIONS · SALT AND PEPPER

Chop the tarragon roughly, then mix with the two mustards and spread the mixture over the chicken. Fry the chicken thoroughly on all sides, in a casserole with olive oil, over low heat.

Wash and scrub the potatoes well. Slice the lemon and add to the casserole with the water/stock. Cover and simmer for 30 minutes.

Add the cream, salt and pepper to taste, and more mustard if necessary. Simmer an additional 15-20 minutes, until the chicken is cooked.

Split the cucumber lengthwise and discard the seeds with a spoon. Cut into 1/2cm slices. Rinse the spring onions, and cut them into sticks of about 3cm. Add the cucumber and spring onion to the casserole and let it simmer for about five minutes.

Serve in the casserole with bread.

GRILLED LAMB RUMP

WITH FRENCH TARRAGON AND CAULIFLOWER POTATO SALAD

SERVES 4

500-600G LAMB RUMP (APPROX. 2 PIECES) · 4-5 SPRIGS ROSEMARY · ½ ORGANIC LEMON
1 TBS OLIVE OIL · SALT AND BLACK PEPPER

POTATO SALAD: 800G SMALL NEW POTATOES · 500 ML CRÈME FRAÎCHE OR PLAIN YOGHURT
2 TSP DIJON MUSTARD · 2 TSP WHOLEGRAIN MUSTARD · 1 RED ONION, FINELY CHOPPED
200G CAULIFLOWER · 1 TBS LEMON JUICE · SALT AND FRESHLY-GROUND BLACK PEPPER
1/4 BUNCH OR 10G TARRAGON

Score the fat on the lamb rumps with a sharp knife. Chop the rosemary finely, grate the lemon rind finely, then mix both with oil, lemon juice, salt and pepper to make your marinade. Marinate the meat while preparing the potatoes.

Scrub the new potatoes and cook until tender in lightly-salted water. Leave to cool, then cut into slices. Break or cut the cauliflower into small florets.

Stir the mustard, finely chopped red onion and lemon juice into the crème fraîche. Add salt and pepper to taste. Chop the tarragon leaves and turn the whole mix into a bowl.

Cook the lamb rumps on a hot grill pan for 10-15 minutes, or bake in an oven at 200°C/400°F/ Gas Mark 6 for approx. 20-25 minutes. Let the meat rest for 5 minutes.

Serve the lamb with the potato salad.

{ The potato salad goes well with all grilled meat and fish. }

SLICED PORTERHOUSE STEAK

WITH ASPARAGUS AND ONION COMPOTE

SERVES 4

500G PORTERHOUSE, SIRLOIN OR FILLET STEAK · 1 TBSP OLIVE OIL · 16 GREEN ASPARAGUS SPEARS

ONION COMPOTE: 150G RED ONIONS · 12 FRESH ROSEMARY SPRIGS OR ½ TSP DRIED ROSEMARY
1 TBS OLIVE OIL · 1 TSP GRANULATED SUGAR · 2 TBS WHITE VINEGAR · SALT AND BLACK PEPPER

Rinse, halve and chop the onions coarsely, then cook for five minutes in a hot frying pan with rosemary and sugar. Add the vinegar and reduce down. Add salt and pepper to taste.

Season the meat with salt and pepper, brown in a pan, and cook in a pre-heated oven at 200°C/400°F/Gas Mark 6 for 20-25 minutes. Let the meat rest for about 10 minutes.

Cut the meat in slices and serve with the onion compote and steamed asparagus.

MONKFISH

WITH ROSEMARY AND GARLIC WITH TOMATO HERB SALAD

SERVES 4

400G MONKFISH, FILLET OR CHEEK • 4 SPRIGS FRESH ROSEMARY • 2 CLOVES GARLIC
2 TBS OLIVE OIL • SALT AND PEPPER

SALAD: 400G TOMATOES, 3 DIFFERENT VARIETIES • ¼ BUNCH OR 10G CHIVES • ¼ BUNCH OR 10G DILL
½ RED ONION, SLICED • 1 TBS SHERRY VINEGAR /CIDER VINEGAR • 2 TBS OLIVE OIL • ½ TSP SUGAR

Cut the fish into 2cm square pieces. Chop the rosemary and garlic finely, and mix with the olive oil, salt and pepper to make the marinade. Marinate the fish while you make the salad.

Cut the tomatoes into bite-size pieces, chop the herbs finely, add the onion and combine in a bowl. Add the sherry/cider vinegar, olive oil and sugar. Mix well and season to taste with salt and black pepper.

Cook the fish in a hot non-stick frying pan for about one minute on each side. Serve in a bowl or dish over the tomato salad.

 Most types of firm white fish can be substituted for monkfish in this recipe.

RHUBARB AND STRAWBERRY TRIFLE

WITH TOASTED RYE BREAD AND VANILLA CREAM

DESSERT - SERVES 4

400G RHUBARB · 2 SLICES RYE BREAD · 100G ORGANIC GRANULATED CANE SUGAR · ½ VANILLA POD
300ML CREAM · 2 TBS ICING SUGAR · 300G STRAWBERRIES

Clean the rhubarb stalks and cut them into 3cm pieces. Bake at 130°C/250°F/Gas Mark ½ for approximately 15 minutes, or until they are tender, cool then refrigerate. Cut the rye bread into small cubes, then grill in a dry pan until golden. Sprinkle over the cane sugar and allow the bread to caramelise, cool then refrigerate.

Scrape the seeds out of the vanilla pod, and combine with the cream and the icing sugar. Whip the mixture until the texture is light and creamy. Rinse the strawberries, remove the tops and cut them into small pieces, and mix with the cooked rhubarb pieces.

Portion the fruit into four bowls and top with the vanilla cream. Sprinkle with grilled rye bread.

{ Macaroons can be used instead of the caramelised bread cubes. Lightly roast about 16 large macaroons in a pan, then crush them coarsely. }

PAVLOVA

WITH SUMMER BERRIES AND VANILLA CREAM

DESSERT - SERVES 6-8

5 EGG WHITES · 1 PINCH SALT · 350G CASTER SUGAR · 2 TSP VINEGAR · 250ML SINGLE CREAM
1 TBS ICING SUGAR · 500G RASPBERRIES

Put the egg whites in a large mixing bowl with a pinch of salt. Whip until they begin to stiffen. Gradually whisk in the sugar and vinegar until the egg whites are stiff enough to retain their shape when the bowl is turned upside down. Place a heaped spoonful of the whipped egg whites onto a baking sheet covered with baking paper. Repeat until there are four meringues in all.

Bake the meringues for about two hours at 110°C/225°F/Gas Mark ¼. Turn off the oven and let the meringues cool inside. Whip the cream with icing sugar, then fold in half of the raspberries. Spread the mixture over the four meringues, and sprinkle with the remaining raspberries.

 It is easier to handle the meringues using a wet spoon.
Depending on the occasion, you can make one large meringue (to serve more than four people) instead of four small ones.
Almost all types of berries and fruits can be used in this dessert, allowing for countless variations. If you're wondering why vinegar is included in this recipe, its acidity adds a delicious contrast to the sweetness of the dessert.

AUTUMN

HOKKAIDO PUMPKIN SOUP

WITH COCONUT MILK AND CORIANDER SALSA

SERVES 4

500G HOKKAIDO PUMPKIN, BUTTERNUT SQUASH OR SMALL PUMPKIN · 4 LARGE POTATOES
3 CLOVES GARLIC · 2 ONIONS · 2 TBS OLIVE OIL · 2 TSP THYME · 1 GREEN CHILLI
2 CANS COCONUT MILK · 300ML WATER · 2 TBS LEMON JUICE · SALT AND BLACK PEPPER

SALSA: 1 TBS CORIANDER · 1 TBS OLIVE OIL · 1 RED CHILLI · 1-2 TBS TOASTED SESAME SEEDS

Peel and cut the vegetables roughly. Fry them lightly in olive oil with the thyme and chopped green chilli. Add coconut milk and water, and simmer 30-45 minutes. Blend the soup and add lemon juice, salt and pepper to taste.

Sprinkle the hot soup with finely chopped coriander, sliced red chilli and the toasted sesame seeds. Serve with bread.

{ For a variation on this fresh and delicious autumn soup, substitute sweet potatoes, carrots, celery, parsnip or other root vegetables. }

NORDIC OYSTERS

WITH APPLES, PEARL BARLEY, PARSLEY AND CIDER VINEGAR

APPETISER – SERVES 4

12 OYSTERS · 80G PEARL BARLEY · 1 APPLE, CUT INTO SMALL CUBES · 2 SPRIGS FLAT-LEAF PARSLEY
2 TBS CIDER VINEGAR · 2 TBS OLIVE OIL · SALT AND FRESHLY-GROUND BLACK PEPPER

Cook the pearl barley according to the directions on the pack, then leave to cool. Open the 12 oysters (or ask your local fishmonger to do this). Combine the pearl barley with the cubed apple, finely chopped parsley, vinegar and oil. Add salt and pepper to taste.

Serve the oysters on a platter and top each with a teaspoon of the apple mixture.

GRILLED BREAD

WITH MIXED MUSHROOMS, LEMON AND PARMESAN

SERVES 4

4 SLICES DAY-OLD, WHEAT BREAD · 1 CLOVE GARLIC · 2 TBS OLIVE OIL
200G MIXED MUSHROOMS, E.G. PORCINI, PORTOBELLO, CHESTNUT, BROWN-CAP
¼ BUNCH OR 10G FLAT-LEAF PARSLEY · 1 LEMON · SALT AND PEPPER

TO SERVE: PARMESAN CHEESE

Grill or toast the bread until it is crispy. Rub the bread with garlic, then brush with olive oil.

Slice the mushrooms , and flash-fry them in a hot pan with olive oil. Season with salt and pepper. Add lemon juice and lemon zest to taste. Spread the mushrooms over the bread, sprinkle with chopped parsley, and serve with lemon and grated parmesan.

BEETROOT TART

WITH SPELT, GOAT'S CHEESE AND BASIL

SERVES 4-6

200G COOKED AND PEELED BEETROOT · 20 BASIL LEAVES · 4 MEDIUM EGGS · 250ML WHIPPING CREAM
150G GOAT'S CHEESE · SALT AND PEPPER

PASTRY: 100G RYE FLOUR · 100G SPELT FLOUR · 75G BUTTER · 2 TBS WATER · 1 TSP SALT

Combine the flours, salt and water in a blender, and crumble in the butter. Instead of blending the dough, it can also be done by hand by combining all the ingredients and binding them with low fat greek yoghurt. Let the dough rest in the refrigerator for two hours, then roll it out and line the pie dish.

Cut the cooked beetroot into slices, chop the basil coarsely, then combine and spread throughout the pie dish.

Whisk the eggs and cream together with salt and pepper, and pour into the dish. Sprinkle the goat's cheese over the filling. Bake the tart in an oven pre-heated to 180°C/350°F/Gas Mark 4 for 45-55 minutes, or until the tart is golden.

Serve warm or cold with a green salad.

{ Tomatoes or squash can be used instead of beetroot as a variation to this dish. Low fat greek yoghurt is only used if you make the pastry by hand. It's not needed if you follow the recipe using a blender. }

BRAISED PHEASANT PAPPARDELLE

WITH ROOT VEGETABLES, THYME AND WHITE WINE

SERVES 4

1 DRESSED PHEASANT, PLUCKED AND DRAWN · 2 TBS OLIVE OIL · 1 ONION · 2 CARROTS
¼ CELERIAC · 2 GARLIC CLOVES · 6 BAY LEAVES · ½ BUNCH OR 15G THYME
400ML MEDIUM WHITE WINE · 250ML WHIPPING CREAM · 400G PAPPARDELLE PASTA
50G PARMESAN CHEESE · SALT AND BLACK PEPPER

Brown the pheasant well in a casserole with some oil. Wash, peel and roughly cut the vegetables, then add to the casserole and brown lightly. Add the herbs and white wine and bring to the boil. Turn down the heat and simmer for 10 minutes, until the alcohol has evaporated. Pour in the cream, cover and simmer again for an additional 45 minutes. Remove the pheasant and vegetables, and strain off the liquid reserving for later.

Remove the meat from the bones of the pheasant and blend with the vegetables, in a blender, until it becomes a coarse purée/meat sauce. Heat the blended mixture with the liquid from the casserole, and add salt and pepper to taste.

Cook the pasta according to the directions on the pack, and serve it with the pheasant sauce directly from the casserole.

Sprinkle with grated parmesan.

{ Chicken and rabbit are good alternatives when pheasant is out of season. }

FRIED COD

WITH CHORIZO, BRUSSELS SPROUTS, JERUSALEM ARTICHOKES AND ROSEMARY

SERVES 4

400G COD FILLET · 500G JERUSALEM ARTICHOKES, QUARTERED · 250G BRUSSEL SPROUTS, HALVED
150G CHORIZO SAUSAGE · 4 SPRIGS ROSEMARY · 2 CLOVES GARLIC · 1 ONION · 2 TBS OLIVE OIL
SALT AND FRESHLY-GROUND BLACK PEPPER

Mince the garlic and onion, and brown in a pan with 1 tbs olive oil. Add the artichokes and
Brussel sprouts, and cook for 7-8 minutes over medium heat.

Slice the sausage and chop the rosemary coarsely. Combine in the pan for the last 3-4 minutes.
Add salt and pepper to taste.

Cut the fish into four pieces. Fry in a hot pan with 1 tbs olive oil for a minute on each side.
Take the pan off the heat and let the fish rest in the pan for about three minutes.

Serve the fish with the sautéed vegetables and chorizo with accompaniments of rice or bread.

{ You can easily use other types of fish in this tasty autumn dish – and a
pork chop or chicken breast would also make a delicious variation. }

NORDIC BURGER

WITH BEETROOT SALSA, RED ONION AND WHOLEGRAIN MUSTARD MAYO

SERVES 4

800G GROUND BEEF · 6 SPRIGS THYME · SALT AND BLACK PEPPER · 4 BURGER BUNS

BEETROOT SALSA: 100G PICKLED BEETROOTS · 30G CAPERS · 1 RED ONION

WHOLEGRAIN MUSTARD MAYO: 3 TBS MAYONNAISE · 2 TBS WHOLEGRAIN MUSTARD
15G ROASTED HAZELNUTS

To make the salsa – peel and chop the red onion, dice the beetroots, add the capers and mix together. Season with salt and pepper.

To make the wholegrain mustard mayo - Chop the hazelnuts finely. Stir the mustard and nuts into the mayonnaise and set to one side.

To make the burgers - Chop the thyme finely and blend into the ground beef before dividing into 4 portions. Pat them with your hands until you have four firm balls. Then pat them flat and form them into burger patties. Season with salt and pepper.

Fry the burgers in a hot pan with 1tbs olive oil for about two minutes on each side. Warm the burger buns in the oven, and spread with the mustard mayonnaise. Place the patties on the bottom bun, and top with beetroot salsa.

{ The burger would work well accompanied by a fried egg (sunny side up) and chips. }

RUSTIC BREAD

BAKED IN A CAST IRON CASSEROLE WITH WHEAT GRAIN AND SEA SALT

1 BREAD

125G WHEAT GRAIN · 15G FRESH YEAST · 500ML WATER · 1 TBS SALT · 1 TBS HONEY
2 TBS OLIVE OIL · 500G WHEAT FLOUR · 200G SPELT FLOUR

Boil the wheat grain for 20 minutes until tender and cool down. Stir the yeast into a large bowl of water, then add the salt, honey and oil. Gradually add the flour and wheat grain. Knead the dough until it becomes elastic, then put it in a big pot, cover, and let it rest in the refrigerator for at least six hours, or overnight.

Take out the bread and let it rest at room temperature for two hours. In the same pot, bake the bread in a pre-heated oven at 220°C/425°F/Gas Mark 7 for 35-40 minutes. Allow to cool for five minutes before serving.

 The dough can also be used to make rustic rolls: Wet your hands before handling the dough. Cover a baking sheet with baking paper, tear off large dollops of the dough and place them on the sheet. Bake at 200°C/400°F/Gas Mark 6 for about 10 minutes.

NORDIC APPLE TART

WITH CINNAMON AND CRÈME FRAÎCHE

DESSERT - SERVES 8

SWEET SHORTCRUST PASTRY: 400G PLAIN FLOUR · 200G BUTTER, CUBED · 100G ICING SUGAR
3 EGG YOLKS

TART FILLING: 6 SWEET APPLES, APPROXIMATELY 800G · 300 ML CRÈME FRAÎCHE · 100G SUGAR
2 TBS GROUND CINNAMON · 50G FLAKED ALMONDS

Rub the flour and butter together, add sugar and egg yolks, and combine the mixture into a
dough. Wrap the dough in cling film and refrigerate for two hours.
Dust the table top with flour, and roll out the dough with a rolling-pin.
Roll out the pastry and line a tart dish or springform tin with a removable base (approx. 30cm
in diameter). Prick the pastry with a fork, and refrigerate for about an hour.

Wash the apples, peel and remove the core and cut into wedges. Place the apples in a bowl
with the crème fraîche. Mix the sugar and cinnamon, and chop the almonds coarsely.

Fill the tart crust with the apples and crème fraîche, and sprinkle with cinnamon sugar and
almonds.

Bake on the middle shelf of a pre-heated oven at 180°C/350°F/Gas Mark 4 for about 60 minutes.

Serve warm with vanilla ice cream

WINTER

HERRING

WITH DIJON MUSTARD IN DILL BRINE

SERVES 4

8 DOUBLE HERRING FILLETS · 2 TBS DIJON MUSTARD · ½ BUNCH OR 15G DILL · ½ TSP CINNAMON
100G WHEAT/RYE FLOUR · 2 TBS VEGETABLE OIL · 1 TBS BUTTER
SALT AND FRESHLY-GROUND BLACK PEPPER

BRINE: 4 BAY LEAVES · 4 SPRIGS THYME · 400ML HOUSEHOLD VINEGAR · 200G SUGAR
2-3 ONIONS, SLICED · 1 SLICED CARROT · 10 BLACK PEPPERCORNS · SALT

Combine all the brining ingredients in a pot, bring to the boil and add salt to taste. Simmer
for 15 minutes. Spread out the herring fillets on a large chopping board, and sprinkle with
cinnamon, salt and pepper. Coat the fish with mustard and then the dill. Close the fillets on
themselves and turn in flour. Heat the oil with the butter in a non-stick frying pan and fry the
coated fish for about a minute on each side. Place in a casserole and pour the hot brine over
the top. Let the fish soak for at least 6 hours, but preferably 12 hours or more. The herring can
be eaten hot or cold. They can be heated in the brine or in an oven for about five minutes.
Traditionally served with schnapps and cold pilsners.

 Other firm, filleted fish can be substituted, such as trout or mackerel.

SMOKED DUCK

WITH WINTER SALAD, WATERCRESS, POMEGRANATE, CITRUS FRUIT AND CINNAMON YOGHURT

SERVES 4

1 SMOKED DUCK BREAST · 1 HEAD OF CHICORY · 1 BUNCH OR 30G WATERCRESS
100ML POMEGRANATE SEEDS · 1 LARGE ORANGE OR 1 GRAPEFRUIT · 2 TBS OLIVE OIL
100ML NATURAL YOGHURT · 1 TSP GROUND CINNAMON · SALT AND PEPPER

Carve the duck breast lengthwise, in thin slices. Divide the chicory, and mix it with the watercress and pomegranate seeds in a salad bowl.

Peel the orange removing the pith. Chop into small pieces and mix with the oil, yoghurt, salt and pepper.

Stir the cinnamon into the yoghurt, and add salt to taste.

Arrange the salad with duck breast and cinnamon yoghurt. Serve with bread.

NORDIC BRUSCHETTA

WITH CRAB, BORLOTTI BEANS AND FENNEL SALAD

SERVES 4

200G PREPARED CRAB MEAT · 400G CAN BORLOTTI BEANS · 1 FENNEL BULB
½ BUNCH OR 15G FLAT-LEAF PARSLEY · 4 SLICES WHEAT BREAD · 1 GARLIC CLOVE · 2 TBS OLIVE OIL
JUICE OF 1 LEMON · 1 LEMON · SALT AND FRESHLY-GROUND PEPPER

Rinse the beans in cold water. Mix the crab meat, beans and thinly-sliced fennel. Add the olive oil, lemon juice, salt and pepper to taste. Finally, fold the coarsely-chopped parsley into the mix.

Grill the bread until it is brown and crispy, then rub it with garlic.

Spread the crab salad on the four slices of bread, and serve with a lemon wedge.

{ Substituting cooked and shelled prawns or tiger prawns for the crab meat is a good way to vary this fresh appetiser. }

MUSSELS STEAMED

WITH NORDIC WINTER VEGETABLES AND BEER

SERVES 4

2 KG FRESH MUSSELS · 1 ONION · 1 CLOVE GARLIC · 2 CARROTS · 200G WHITE TURNIP
¼ BUNCH OR 10G CURLY-LEAF PARSLEY · 2 TBS OLIVE OIL · 330ML PILSNER BEER
SALT AND FRESHLY-GROUND PEPPER

Clean the mussels thoroughly in cold running water, and discard all those that are damaged.
You can check to see whether the open mussels are still alive by tapping them on the table –
if they don't close up, they should be discarded.

Coarsely chop the onion, garlic, root vegetables and parsley. Heat the oil in a casserole, add
the mussels, and turn in the oil. Add all the vegetables and parsley, then pour the beer into the
casserole. Bring to the boil. Put the lid on,turn down the heat to a low simmer and cook for a
couple of minutes, or until the mussels open. Serve with a sprinkle of salt, pepper and
wholegrain bread.

Discard any mussels which have not opened after cooking.

SPELTOTTO

WITH MUSHROOMS, ROOT VEGETABLES, HERBS AND APPLES

SERVES 4

4 STICKS CELERY · 2 CARROTS · 1 LEEK · 1 ONION · 2 CLOVES GARLIC · 3 TBS OLIVE OIL
25G DRIED PORCINI MUSHROOMS, SOAKED · 250G PEARLED SPELT OR WHEAT KERNELS
300ML WHEAT BEER · 500ML CHICKEN STOCK · 150G CUBED BUTTER · 100G GRATED PARMESAN
1 GREEN APPLE, CUT INTO CUBES · CELERY LEAVES · SALT AND BLACK PEPPER

Cut all the vegetables and the mushrooms finely. In a pot, fry the vegetables gently in the olive oil, without colouring. Fold the spelt into the vegetables. Cook 3-4 minutes over a low heat while stirring, until the spelt has absorbed the oil. Pour in the beer and reduce almost completely, until the smell of alcohol is gone.

Bring the chicken stock to a boil in a separate saucepan. Pour over the spelt little by little, over a low heat, stirring continuously.

Repeat this process for about 20 minutes, until the spelt is tender. When the spelt is done, but is still al dente, fold the cubed butter and 50g parmesan into the pot. Add salt and pepper to taste. The speltotto should be soft and almost fluid.

Serve the speltotto on warm plates or in petite casseroles with the apple cubes, celery leaves and remaining 50g of grated parmesan. Accompany with a wheat beer.

{ Substitute Carnaroli rice for pearled spelt to get a risotto version of this dish. You can also use pearl barley or other whole, fine grains instead of pearled spelt. }

POTATO & LEEK GRATIN

WITH BACON, CRISPY BREADCRUMBS AND THYME

SERVES 4

1 KG LEEKS · 400G BACON · 1 KG WHITE POTATOES, MASHED · 2 TBS THYME · 80G BREADCRUMBS
50G PARMESAN CHEESE · 100G GRATED MOZZARELLA CHEESE · SALT AND CRUSHED BLACK PEPPER

Wash and cut the leeks in 3cm rounds. Cut the bacon into 3cm square pieces, and fry in
a dry, non-stick frying pan until golden and crispy. Combine the bacon and leeks in an
oven safe casserole and season with salt and pepper. Top with mashed potatoes, and mix
the breadcrumbs,cheese and thyme and sprinkle on top. Bake in a pre-heated oven at
200°C/400°F/Gas Mark 6 for 35-40 minutes, until the surface is golden and crispy.

NORDIC WINTER STIR-FRY

WITH BEEF, ROOT VEGETABLES AND GINGER

SERVES 4

400G SIRLOIN BEEF · 400G ROOT VEGETABLES: PARSNIPS, CARROTS AND CELERY · 50G GINGER
200ML OYSTER SAUCE · 1 ONION · 2 CLOVES GARLIC · 2 TBS SUNFLOWER OIL
¼ BUNCH OR 10G CORIANDER · SALT AND FRESHLY-GROUND BLACK PEPPER

Cut the ginger into fine strips, and coarsely chop the garlic and onion.
Peel the root vegetables, and cut them lengthwise into thin slices with a mandolin slicer
or peeler. Cut the beef into strips. Heat the oil in the wok, stir-fry the beef and push to the
sides of the wok. Add the onions and garlic followed by the vegetables and stir-fry for about
2 minutes. Combine the meat with the vegetables and stir in the oyster sauce. Adjust the
seasoning to taste with salt and pepper. Sprinkle with chopped coriander, and serve the dish
with noodles or rice.

BRAISED PORK CHEEKS

WITH HERBS, RED WINE AND ROOT-VEGETABLES

SERVES 4

600G PORK CHEEKS · 2 TBS VEGETABLE OIL · 1 TBS TOMATO PURÉE · 4 CLOVES GARLIC
½ TSP CRUSHED BLACK PEPPER · ½ BOTTLE RED WINE · 500ML WATER · 10 BAY LEAVES
6 SPRIGS THYME · 25G DRIED PORCINI MUSHROOMS, SOAKED · 3 CARROTS, SLICED
2 ONIONS, CHOPPED · 2 CELERY STICKS, SLICED · 1 TSP SALT

Clean the pork cheeks and flash-fry in a pot with the oil. Add tomato purée, garlic and black pepper. Cook for about two minutes. Pour in the red wine and simmer for 10 minutes. Add the soaked mushrooms, thyme and bay leaves along with the water and simmer for another hour. Add the carrots, onion and celery sticks and simmer for another 30 minutes, until the meat is tender. Add salt to taste.

Serve the dish in the pot, with mashed potatoes or rice and bread.

STEAK SANDWICH

WITH ROASTED PEPPER SALSA, ONIONS AND GRILLED BREAD

SERVES 4

500G FILLET OF BEEF IN 4 STEAKS • 1 TBS OLIVE OIL • 200G ROASTED RED PEPPER • 2 TBS CAPERS
20 BASIL LEAVES • 1 TBS OLIVE OIL • 2 TSP CIDER VINEGAR • SALT • BLACK PEPPER
1 RED ONION • ½ HEAD LETTUCE, ICEBERG • 2-3 TBS MAYONNAISE • 8 SLICES GRILLED BREAD

Chop the roasted pepper coarsely. Mix with the capers, finely-cut basil, olive oil and vinegar.
Add salt and pepper to taste.

Fry the beef or steak in a hot cast iron frying pan with the vegetable oil for about two minutes
on each side, then let it rest for 5-10 minutes. Spread the mayonnaise on the bread. Build up
the sandwich with lettuce, meat, pepper salsa, and top with sliced red onion.

Can be served with chips.

 Roasted peppers can be purchased in jars in most supermarkets.
Alternatively, you can make your own by cutting 300g red pepper
into large flat pieces, and grilling them in the oven at 200°C/400°F/
Gas Mark 6 until the skin blackens, and the pepper is soft all the way
through. Leave to cool then peel off skin.

CHRISTMAS ICE CREAM

WITH MARZIPAN, NUTS, CHOCOLATE AND CHERRIES

DESSERT - SERVES 6-8

3 PASTEURISED EGG WHITES · 60G ICING SUGAR · 500ML WHIPPING CREAM · 50G MARZIPAN
50G CHOCOLATE, 60-70% COCOA SOLIDS · 50G NOUGAT · 30G ALMONDS
PICKLED CHERRIES OR GROUND CINNAMON

Whisk the egg whites and the icing sugar until stiff. Gently whip the cream, then fold into the whipped egg whites. Chop the marzipan, chocolate, nougat and nuts coarsely, then carefully fold into the mixture. Pour into a freezer safe dish. Freeze for at least six hours. Remove from the freezer and stand at room temperature for 10 minutes prior to serving.

Serve with pickled cherries or a dusting of ground cinnamon.

HONEY HEARTS

WITH ICING

MAKES APPROX. 10 HEARTS

75G HONEY · 75G BROWN SUGAR · 60G BUTTER · 1 LARGE EGG · 1 TSP GROUND CINNAMON
½ TSP GROUND CLOVE · ½ TSPN BAKING SODA · 300G PLAIN FLOUR PLUS EXTRA FOR ROLLING

ICING: 1 EGG WHITE · 5 TBS ICING SUGAR

Melt together the honey, brown sugar and butter in a saucepan. Pour the mixture into a small bowl. When it has had time to cool, mix in the egg and the dry ingredients. Mix well.

Knead the dough on a clean table dusted with flour. Allow the dough to rest for 1 hour, then roll it out until it is about ½ centimetre thick. Remember to dust with flour, so the dough doesn't stick to the table. Shape the honey hearts with a heart-shaped pastry cutter.

Place the honey hearts on a baking sheet lined with baking paper. Bake in a pre-heated oven at 200°C/400°F/Gas Mark 6 for about 10 minutes, or until they are golden and crispy.

Make the icing while the hearts are in the oven. Whisk the icing sugar and the egg white together thoroughly, so there are no lumps. Cool the hearts on a cooling tray before glazing.

BISCOTTI

COOKIES WITH ALMONDS

MAKES 20-25

160G SHELLED WHOLE ALMONDS · 350G WHEAT FLOUR · 250G CANE SUGAR · 1 TSP BAKING POWDER
3 EGGS · 90G DARK CHOCOLATE COARSELY CHOPPED, OPTIONAL · EGG WHITES FOR BRUSHING

Bake the almonds in a pre-heated oven at 170°C/325°F/Gas Mark 3 until they are golden (this takes about 20 minutes). Allow to cool. Blend half of the nuts finely in a processor. Add flour, sugar, baking powder and mix. Add the eggs into the mixture one at a time. Fold in the rest of the almonds and the coarsely-chopped chocolate (optional). Form the dough into two oblong "sausages" and place them onto a baking sheet covered with baking paper. Brush with the egg whites. Cool for one hour.

Bake in a pre-heated oven at 180°C/350°F/Gas Mark 4 for about 25 minutes. Cool for a few moments before slicing each roll into 10-12 pieces. Bake the sliced biscotti in a pre-heated oven at 150°C/300°F/Gas Mark 2 for 30-40 minutes, until they are crispy and slightly golden. Let the finished biscotti cool.

Store in an air tight container.

THE SCANDINAVIAN WAY TO COOK
© Niche Books 2012

PUBLISHED FOR:

Le Creuset UK Ltd
83 Livingstone Road
Walworth Business Park
Andover
Hampshire
SP10 5QZ

PUBLISHER:

Niche Books aps
Godthåbsvej 34B
DK-2000 Frederiksberg
www.nichebooks.dk

EDITOR:

Anders Borggaard Pajor

RECIPES & STYLING:

Carsten Kyster

PHOTOGRAPHY:

Maria P

DESIGN & LAYOUT:

Niche Group

PRINT:

Clemenstrykkeriet A/S